A Mormon Cookbook

Food, Facts & Friendship
by Erin A. Delfoe

The American Pantry Collection™

Published by:
Apricot Press
Box 1611
American Fork, Utah
84003

books@apricotpress.com
www.apricotpress.com

ISBN 1-885027-16-8

Cover & Design by David Mecham
Printed in the United States of America

Forward

The other day, I was reading a magazine with one of my roommates and an article caught my eye. The article described the, "Top Ten Healthiest Cities in the United States." To our surprise, number one was Provo, Utah. My friend and I looked at each other and yelled, "All Right! We live in Provo! We'll live to be 150!"

Most likely, the reason Provo is so healthy is because of all the Mormons who live here. I have been a Mormon my whole life, and I'm here to tell you that we have our own way of doing things, our own culture. It's this lifestyle that has earned us the title of the healthiest people in the world. I'd like to share with you some of the reasons why we're so healthy. Many people consider us a bit peculiar, but by sharing with you some of what we eat, and what we do, hopefully you can come to understand us better.

Now that we have all of that out of the way, we can move on to the more important stuff, or at least the better tasting stuff, THE FOOD!

About the Author –

Erin Allred is a descendent of true Mormon pioneer stock. Her ancestors on both sides of the family were among the original western pioneers.

Some of them made the trek from Nauvoo, Illinois, to Salt Lake City, Utah, by wagon train. Others made the perilous journey from the east cost around Cape Horn by ship to San Francisco, then on to Utah by wagon train.

She is the author of a cooking column titled, "What's cooking in Erin's kitchen" and is also the author of the cook book "Hot Cooking, Recipes for those who just can't get it hot enough." Erin also made contributions to the book "Understanding Women."

Erin will graduate this year with a degree in journalism from Brigham Young University.

RECIPES

Utah's Famous Green Jello with Cheese   8

Funeral Potatoes   10

Joseph Smith's Ginger Snaps   14

Famous Utah Pink Sauce   16

Mormon Pioneer Apple Crisp   18

Great Salt Lake Vinegar Taffy   20

Wasatch Whole Wheat Bread   22

Missouri River Mud Pie   26

Rice Crispy Treats   28

Mormon Battalion 5-hour Stew   30

Word of Wisdom Waffles   32

Frontier Bacon with Garden Peas   33

Brother Brigham's Pumpkin Roll   34

Grandma Great's Rice Pudding   36

Bishop's Baby Carrots with Pineapple Glaze 38

Missionaries' Favorite Lasagna 40

Mushy Missionary Oatmeal Cookies 42

-- Quick Ideas --

Pioneer Bread and Milk 45

Cucumbers in Vinegar 46

Short-Cut Rice Pudding 47

Apple Slices in Peanut Butter 48

Anytime Cinnamon Toast 49

Basic Boiled Squash 50

Garden Radishes and Salt 50

Campfire Caramel Popcorn 51

Yummy Fruit Dip 52

Green Onion & Cheese Appetizers 53

TCT's 54

Frontier Style Boiled Wheat 55

Trail-side Granola Mix   57

Pioneer Baked Beans   58

Wagon Train Oatmeal Muffins   60

Original Pioneer Soda Biscuits   62

Stick to Your Ribs Working Pancakes   63

Grandma Fawn's Dumplings   64

The Relief Society's 5 Cup Salad   66

Hotel Utah Rolls   68

Polygamist Potato Pancakes   70

The Allred Family Broccoli Casserole   74

Family Home Evening Rhubarb Pie   76

Relief Society Macaroni Casserole   78

Book of Mormon Meat Pie   79

Grandpa's Grape Jelly   80

Mormon Miracle Turkey Dressing   82

Utah's famous
Green Jello With Cheese

1/2 cup crushed pineapple	1 3oz. package lime Jell-O
1/2 cup water	1 cup grated cheese
2/3 cup sugar	1 cup whipped cream

   Mix first 3 ingredients together. Boil 1 cup water. Add 1 package lime jello to water. Add mixture to jello and let set until wobbly. Add 1 cup grated cheese, 1 cup whipped cream and mix. Then let finish setting.

This first dish may not be proven to ward off heart disease or cancer, but Mormons, for some unknown reason, have long been known for their consumption of Jell-O, especially green Jell-O. It is something of a joke among members because at every church function it shows up in some form or another. People have become so creative with their Jell-O recipes that it is not uncommon to find ingredients such as carrots, marshmallows, cheese, nuts and other little extras, that most people would never think to put in a Jell-O mold, gracing tables at almost every Mormon gathering.

Now, I know that some of these Jell-O additives may sound a little strange, but the one rule that cooks and food connoisseurs alike must live by is, "Don't knock it 'till you've tried it." Jell-O has become such a tradition in the state, that Utah has named it their official food. This honor comes with many perks such as the official green Jell-O Olympic pin.

Funeral Potatoes

8 medium baked and grated potatoes

1/2 cube melted margarine

2 cans cream of chicken or cream of mushroom soup

1 cup sour cream

1/2 cup shredded cheese

Mix ingredients together.

Crush 2 cups corn flakes, add 2 tablespoons melted butter, and sprinkle over the top. Bake in a 9x13 pan at 350° for 30 minutes.

Another part of Mormon Tradition is a luncheon held at the church after funeral services, (You will find that in most Mormon cultures food is served prior to, during, and immediately after, almost every event).

Now, I know that this may sound a little morbid for a cook book and hopefully, you don't lose your appetite, but in Mormon culture whenever there is a funeral, the Relief Society offers its support and aid to the family of the deceased. Often times they are asked to provide the food for the family dinner that is traditionally held after the funeral service.

Although this dish is brought to almost every pot luck dinner held after funerals, which I suppose is a little unsettling, it is still one of my favorite dishes. Hopefully the deceased, or their families, don't find it offensive when I'm going back for fourth's instead of standing in line to pay my respects.

Little Crumbs of info about the Mormon Church, and its people....

The real name of the Mormon Church is "The Church of Jesus Christ of Latter Day Saints."

Mormons received this nickname from their book of scripture called The Book of Mormon.

The Mormon Church has a "lay" priesthood. That means most members are called to serve in all kinds of capacities and they aren't paid for their services.

The Mormon Church is lead by a man who we consider a prophet, much like Old Testament Prophets, who in turn gets his instructions by revelation from Jesus Christ.

The first such prophet in modern times was Joseph Smith, who had a vision in 1820 where God, the Father, and Jesus Christ appeared to him, giving him instructions to restore Christ's church to the earth as it had been in ancient times.

Joseph Smith, along with his brother, Hyrum, was murdered by a mob in Carthage, Illinois on June 20, 1844.

Joseph Smith's

Gingersnaps

3/4 cup shortening

1 cup brown sugar (packed)

1 egg

1/4 cup molasses

2-1/4 cups all-purpose flour

2 teaspoons soda

1 teaspoon cinnamon

1 teaspoon ginger

1/2 teaspoon cloves

1/4 teaspoon salt

Granulated sugar

Mix thoroughly shortening, brown sugar, egg and molasses. Blend in remaining ingredients except granulated sugar. Cover; chill 1 hour.

Heat oven to 375°. Shape dough by rounded teaspoonfuls into balls. Dip tops in granulated sugar. Place balls, sugared side up, 3 inches apart on lightly greased baking sheet. Bake 10 to 12 minutes or just until set. Immediately remove from baking sheet.

A few more little facts about Mormons to sprinkle on your cereal.

The Mormon organization for women called The Relief Society is both the oldest and largest women's' organization in the United States.

~|~

The purpose of the Mormon Relief Society is to provide compassionate service to women and their families - both Mormon and non-Mormon alike.

~|~

The Relief Society has millions of members from all over making the world a better place.

~|~

Famous Utah
Pink Sauce

This is another famous Utah treat. If you've
ever been to Utah, you may have noticed pink
sauce in all the restaurants.

Pink sauce is a dipping sauce, usually for
french fries, that until recently was only found
in Utah. I don't know who invented it, but
every burger place in Utah has it on their
menu, even McDonalds. The sauce is nothing
more than a mixture of 50% Ketchup and 50%
Mayonnaise, which makes it a pink color
(hence the name). I have been on many a
road trip where we have been out of state and
stopped at McDonalds. The poor kids that
have grown up their whole lives in Utah step
up to the counter and order fries with pink
sauce and the cashier just gives them a
strange look. Those of us who have been out
of state have to explain to them that it's just a
Utah thing, and they end up getting ketchup
and mayonnaise and mixing it themselves. Be
warned, once you've tried this, plain old
Ketchup just won't do.

More yeast for your already rising bread of knowledge about Mormons.

Mormons quietly contribute hundreds of millions of dollars to aid the poorest people in crisis, from refugees in Bosnia to those struggling in Central Africa, to people displaced in Latin America-Mormons and Non-Mormons alike

‿Ⅰ⁀

Besides helping non-Church members in need, the church also has a welfare program to help people close to home. Bishops distribute donations each week to those who are temporarily out of work, ill, or otherwise distressed.

‿Ⅰ⁀

Most of this money comes from member donations saved when once-a-month they fast for two meals and donate the proceeds to the "fast offering" to help the needy.

Mormon Pioneer
Apple Crisp

Mix:

2 cups sugar

5 tablespoons cornstarch

Add:

2 cups water

2 teaspoons vanilla

Cook until clear and thick; pour over 10 cups peeled, sliced apples.

Combine and sprinkle over apples:

1 cup flour

1 cup rolled oats

1-1/2 teaspoons cinnamon

1-1/4 cups brown sugar

3/4 cup melted butter

1/2 cup nuts

Bake at 325° for 1 hour in 9x13 pan.

In 1839, Joseph Smith and other church leaders acquired swampland on the bend in the Mississippi River known as Commerce, Illinois.

\\//

They renamed the swamp Nauvoo and began a city which was to become the largest in Illinois.

\\//

In June, 1844, Joseph and his brother, Hyrum, were murdered by a mob while they awaited a hearing under a guarantee of protection from Illinois governor Ford.

\\//

Leadership of the Church then fell to Brigham Young, the senior member of the twelve Apostles.

\\//

In simpler times, when people wanted something to do that was fun and social and would result in a sweet treat, Mormons would often have a taffy pull. Friends or family would mix up the taffy and then sit for a while and pull it and visit.

My family still does this today. My aunt JoLyn is well known for her delicious taffy. This is her recipe.

Great Salt Lake
Vinegar Taffy

2 cups sugar   3/4 cup water

1/2 cup vinegar   1/8 tsp cream of tartar

Combine ingredients and boil to hard ball stage. Do not stir. Pour on buttered tray and wait until cool to touch. Each "puller" should tear off a piece, then pull and stretch it until it becomes white.

Cut into bite-sized pieces and roll in mixture of 2 Tbs. powdered sugar and 2 Tbs. corn starch.

Wasatch Whole Wheat
Bread

**1 pkg. dry yeast
(1 tablespoon)**

3 cups warm water

1 cup white flour

1 cup oatmeal

1/4 cup molasses

**6 Tbsps. nonfat
dry milk**

6 Tbsps. shortening

**6-1/2 cups whole
wheat flour**

1-1/2 Tbsps. salt

Dissolve yeast in 1/4 cup lukewarm water. Combine remaining 2-3/4 cups water, oatmeal, molasses, and dry milk; add half the white flour and half the whole wheat flour, one cup at a time, beating well after each.

Add yeast, the remaining flour, shortening, and salt. Mix well, then knead until dough is smooth. Place in covered bowl in warm area until doubled in size. Knead for one minute until air bubbles are forced out. Mold into two loaves of equal size. Place in 2 well-greased bread pans. Cover and let rise until double in size. Bake at 400° for 1 hour. Remove from pans to cool. Brush tops of loaves with butter and serve.

Realizing the Saints could never avoid persecution in the East, Brigham Young led them on an epic journey into the Utah Territory, which was then Mexico.

~|⁄.

In Utah, he began one of the most remarkable and successful colonizations in world history, sending groups of Saints to create nearly 1000 small towns throughout the Mountain West.

~|⁄.

Under Brigham Young's direction, settlements were established in San Bernadino, California, Colonial Juarez, Mexico, throughout Southern Idaho, Utah, Las Vegas, Nevada, and Star Valley, Wyoming.

~|⁄.

Mormonisms

Since the churches humble beginnings with the prophet Joseph Smith, Mormon people have developed their own sub-cultures. If you've ever been around a group of Mormons, you may have noticed that they use certain words and phrases that you probably don't hear anywhere else, Mormonisms, if you will.

I have spent most of my life in the state of Utah and had never realized that Mormons have a different way of speaking until I moved to the state of Washington. I remember people giving me funny looks when I would talk. They would even tell me I had a Utah accent, whatever that meant.

Having lived through that experience, I will shed a little light on some of the words and phrases that Mormons use, and what they mean.

"Oh my heck!": A Mormon expletive used when surprised or astounded.

"Elder": A priesthood office which has specific duties including missionary work.

The term, "Elder" can be confusing because some are just18 year old young men.

"Teacher": Another priesthood office often made up of 14 to 16-year-old boys.

"Priest": A priesthood office authorized to do such things as baptize and conduct meetings.

"Fireside": This is not just a bunch of people sitting around a fire. This is when a group of Mormons get together and listen to a speaker; of course there is usually food.

"Caffeine Free Coke": Yes they do make it.

"Pop": For everyone else in the world, you know it as soda.

"Institute": Classes you can take in college that teach about gospel subjects such as The Bible, Book of Mormon, Prophets, or the ancient church.

"Primary": The organization set up to teach children ages 2 through 12.

Missouri River
Mud Pie

9-inch Graham Cracker Crust

16 large marshmallows or 1-1/2 cups mini marshmallows

1/2 cup milk

3 bars (3.5 oz. bars) milk chocolate

1 cup chilled whipping cream - or 1 envelope (2 oz.) dessert topping mix

Prepare crust. Heat marshmallows, milk and chocolate over medium heat, stirring constantly, just until marshmallows and chocolate melt and blend. Chill until thickened.

In chilled bowl, beat cream until stiff. Stir marshmallow mixture to blend; fold into whipped cream. Pour into crust. Chill at least 8 hours or until set. If desired, garnish with toasted, slivered almonds.

More Mormonisms

"Flip!, Fetch!, or Shoot!": Substitutes for sound alike expletives.

"Stake house": (Not to be confused with "Steak House") A large meeting house wherein are Stake offices and where stake meetings are held. (See Stake)

"Stake": (Not to be confused with steak) A congregation of 2000-5000 members organized into wards of 250-700 members and presided over by three high priests. (The stake presidency).

"Relief Society": The oldest and largest women's' organization in the world; dedicated to service.

"R.M.": Returned Missionary, as in, "She's dating an R.M."

"Singles Ward": This is a Mormon ward with only single adults. One of its main purposes is to put people together so they can meet someone to marry.

Favorite
Rice Crispy Treats

3 tablespoons margarine

4 cups marshmallows

6 cups Rice Krispie cereal

Melt margarine in a large saucepan over low heat. Add marshmallows and stir until melted. Remove from heat.

Add Rice Krispies. Stir until well coated with melted marshmallow / margarine mix.

Using a buttered spatula or waxed paper, press mixture evenly into 9" x 13" buttered pan. Let cool and cut into 2" squares.

This is a quick and delicious treat that always seems to show up at every Mormon function.

Sometimes people get creative and put things like M & M's in them, or mold them into shapes like teddy bears or stars, but most of the time it's just the good old squares right out of the pan.

ⅴ\\⋁⁄ⅴ

Mormon Battalion
5-Hour Stew

4 potatoes, diced

6 carrots, chopped

1 cup celery, chopped

1 onion, chopped

1 green pepper, chopped

1 cup water

2 small cans tomato sauce

2 pounds round steak, cut in 1" squares

1-1/2 teaspoons salt

1/4 teaspoon pepper

Cover and cook 5 hours at 250°.

A Mormon Urban Legend

There is a funny little story that circulates about the Mormon people and one of their temples (maybe you've heard it, too). I was surprised the first time I heard it because I couldn't believe that the person telling it to me actually thought it was true. So, here I am to set the record straight. The story went something like this:

Back in the olden days, when Brigham Young was still alive, he had many wives. (This is the only true part of the story and it will be addressed later in the book.) The legend is, he would capture young girls and lock them up in the top of the Salt Lake temple where they could never escape. One day, Brigham went to the top of the temple to check on his newest captive, and to his surprise, she was nowhere to be found. She had managed to escape by jumping out of one of the windows into the Great Salt Lake, and swimming to safety.

After hearing this story, I was so amazed that anyone could actually believe it that all I could say to the man telling the story was that the Great Salt Lake was about 10 miles from the temple and the girl would have to jump pretty far in order to make it there.

———————— \\//⁄ ————————

Word of Wisdom
Waffles

2 eggs

2 cups buttermilk

2 cups all-purpose flour

2 teaspoons baking powder

1 teaspoon soda

1/2 teaspoon salt

1/4 cup plus 2 tablespoons shortening

Heat waffle iron. Beat eggs; beat in remaining ingredients with rotary beater until smooth.

Pour batter from cup or pitcher onto center of hot waffle iron. Bake about 5 minutes or until steaming stops. Remove waffle carefully.

Frontier Bacon with
Garden Peas

2 cups cooked peas

2 slices bacon

**freshly ground
pepper**

Cut the bacon into small strips and fry
until crisp.

Pour off part of the fat, leaving about 2 tablespoons. Add the cooked drained peas and heat.
Do not boil. Add pepper to taste.

Also good with fresh green beans.

Brother Brigham's
Pumpkin Roll

3 eggs

1 cup sugar

2/3 cup pumpkin

1 teaspoon baking
soda

1 teaspoon
cinnamon

3/4 cup flour

Filling

1-8 oz. pkg.
cream cheese

4 teaspoons
soft butter

1 cup powder sugar

1/2 teaspoon
vanilla

Mix and pour on cookie sheet, bake 10-15 minutes at 350°. Roll and let cool.

Pour onto unrolled cooled cake. Roll and chill.

Make sure you put wax paper on cookie sheet and spray with oil before pouring mix on cookie sheet.

A few more teaspoons of knowledge about Mormons...

Mormons who are worthy to marry in the temple are sealed there with their children to be together for eternity.

Sacred ordinances are also done in temples by proxy for people who have died. For example, baptisms are done for the dead, couples who have passed on are sealed for eternity to each other and to their children.

Because of this commitment to everyone who has ever lived, Mormons lead the world in genealogy work. By contacting a Mormon congregation (also called a Ward or Stake), even if you are not a Mormon, you can receive assistance and have access to their data banks to research your ancestors, normally free of charge.

Grandma Great's
Rice Pudding

1 cup rice, cooked
3 beaten eggs
1/4 cup sugar
cinnamon

1/2 teaspoon vanilla

2-1/2 cups milk

1/4 cup raisins

Mix all together and sprinkle nutmeg on top. Put the pan the pudding is in inside a larger pan of water. Bake at 375° for 1/2 hour. Insert knife in pudding, if it comes out clean, its done.

My Grandparents recently returned from a mission in England where their main purpose was to work in the Mormon Church History Center.

They learned many things, one of which was how to use the church computer system known as "family search" to find people's ancestors. They helped hundreds of visitors find their ancestors.

Many people had been looking for a particular person for many years and my grandparents were able to help find them. There are Church History Centers all over the world, if you have an interest in your family history, find one near you and someone like my grandparents can help you locate those ancestors you've been looking for.

Bishop's Baby Carrots
with Pineapple Glaze

3 cups baby carrots

3 med. leeks, sliced 1/2 inch thick

2 tablespoons water

1-6 oz can (2/3 cup) unsweetened pineapple juice

2 teaspoons cornstarch

1/2 teaspoon grated fresh ginger root or 1/8 teaspoon ground ginger

1/8 teaspoon salt (optional)

1/8 teaspoon ground nutmeg

In a 2 quart microwave safe casserole dish, combine the carrots, leeks, and water and cover. Microwave on high 9 to 11 minutes or until crisp-tender, stirring once. Drain: keep covered to keep warm.

Glaze – In a 2 cup microwave safe measuring dish, combine juice, cornstarch, ginger root, salt, and nutmeg. Cook, uncovered, on high for 2-1/2 to 3-1/2 minutes or until thickened and bubbly, stirring every minute until slightly thickened, then after every 30 seconds. Pour the glaze over carrots; stir to coat. Garnish each serving with a dollop of plain yogurt. Makes 4 servings.

A Mormon Bishop is the ecclesiastical leader of a congregation of between 250 and 700 members. There are currently in excess of 30,000 such bishops in the church spending countless hours looking after their memberships without financial compensation. They do such things as conduct meetings, coordinate aid for the poor, hold temple worthiness interviews, etc.

My grandfather, the same one who recently returned from a mission, was a bishop for many years, and he loves this recipe. I think you will love it too, simply because it's just plain good.

It may also help young children to eat more vegetables because it makes carrots seem more like a candy than a vegetable. Finding something to help kids eat more vegetables is always a plus in any culture. As most everyone knows, many Mormon families are large, so when they buy their carrots in bulk, they better get someone to eat them.

Missionaries' Favorite
Lasagna

2 lbs. ground beef

1 onion, diced

1 quart tomatoes or
tomato puree

1-10 oz. can
tomato soup

1 teaspoon sweet
basil

1/2 teaspoon
oregano

1-8 oz. carton
cottage cheese

1 lb. sliced
Monterey Jack
cheese

Salt and pepper
to taste

Parmesan cheese
to taste

Cook 1-8 oz. package of lasagna noodles for about 12 minutes in boiling water. When finished, soak noodles in cold water until needed. Fry meat, salt, pepper, and onion. Add tomatoes, sauce, soup, basil, and oregano. Simmer on low heat for 20-30 minutes in sauce pan. Assemble ingredients in 9x13x2 pan in 2 layers: noodles, cottage cheese, meat mixture, Parmesan, Monterey Jack cheeses. Top with thin layer of meat mixture and parmesan cheese. Bake uncovered for 25-35 minutes at 375 degrees.

Currently, over 60,000 full-time missionaries are serving throughout the world spreading the gospel at their own expense. Most are missionaries for 18 months to 2 years.

\\//

The majority of these missionaries are young men between the ages of 19 and 25, but there are also large numbers of young women ages 21-25 and retired couples.

\\//

Missionaries must learn many different languages in order to go to work in all the different countries.

\\//

They learn these languages in Missionary Training Centers, with the help of the Lord, in three months.

Mushy Missionary
Oatmeal Cookies

1 cup butter

1/4 cup white sugar

1 teaspoon soda

1-4 oz. pkg. vanilla instant pudding

3-1/2 cups quick cooking oats

2 eggs

3/4 cup brown sugar

1-1/4 cup flour

chocolate chips, nuts, or raisins to taste

Mix butter, sugar and eggs together, then add the remaining ingredients. Bake at 375° for 10 minutes.

More on Mormon Missionaries

There are so many young men on missions today, that one could say that a young woman "waiting for a missionary" has also become a part of Mormon culture. Sometimes 'waiting' lasts only about two to three weeks until the girl meets another classy guy, often times an already returned missionary, and sends the poor guy serving in Guam, or somewhere equally far away, a "Dear John" letter. A "Dear John" is the letter that the girl waiting at home sends her boyfriend out on his mission (Men serving in the Military may also experience the dreaded Dear John letter.) This letter explains to him that she has met someone else and will no longer be writing him any more, much less 'waiting'.

Dear John's may go something like this.

Dear Elder John,
        I'm really very sorry to have to tell you this but remember Tim, your best friend. Well, he just happened to return home from his mission 5-weeks before you, and we started dating. Now we're getting married. Enclosed is our wedding announcement. We scheduled our wedding the day after you get home so you can come.

Love, Sue

P.S. Tim wants to know if you'll be his best man.

Quick Ideas

Mormon Munchies for People on the Go

These quick little treats come from a variety of sources. Some were favorites of my great grandpa, Homer Duncan, after he'd come in from a hard days work on his farm. Others come from my aunt, who needed to quiet her nine children by giving them something good to eat. Some are old pioneer favorites, and others were used to get the young men to show up for a service project. Some are native to the Utah area, and some may have been used by your own family from time to time. Whatever the case may be, pick a few of your favorites from this list and you'll always have something handy.

Pioneer
Bread and Milk

In the early days of the church in Utah, bread and milk was a staple. Nearly all of my ancestors ate it regularly. Because practically everyone farmed and worked long hours, they would have their biggest meal of the day at midday. Then, they would work hard until dark. When they would come home tired at night, they wanted something simple yet good. Bread and milk fit the bill.

I remember Grandpa would just break up a couple of pieces of homemade bread into a bowl and then pour whole milk on it. My grandpa's family usually put jam, jelly or honey on top. On the other hand, my grandma's family ate their bread and milk with slices of cheese and little green onions. My dad still eats it occasionally; he especially likes it with grape jelly.

Cucumbers
in Vinegar

This is a family favorite, which we also learned from my grandmas. It's easy, quick, and healthy.

All you do is peal a cucumber and slice it. drop the slices into a bowl of 1 part vinegar and 1 part water, add a little salt and pepper and let it sit for about an hour. Then, enjoy nibbling on this treat all day long.

This is a great way to use up extra cucumbers from your garden. Some people add tomato wedges to the mix for variety.

Short-cut
Rice Pudding

If you like rice pudding you'll love this faster, simpler version of pretty much the same thing. This is one of my grandma's favorite things. She says it was one of her grandma's favorites, and probably hers before that.

Just add milk to a bowl of hot, cooked rice, just like you would cold cereal. then, simply sprinkle on some sugar and cinnamon. Voila!

———— //\\/\\/\\ ————

Apple Slices &
Peanut Butter

This is the classic nursery treat. The nursery is the Sunday class for all the kids 18 months to 3 years old. (That's the class most people pray they don't get asked to teach!)

Cut up some apple slices, spread peanut butter on them and put them on a plate. Usually it will stop the little kids from fussing – at least until they finish chewing it!

Anytime
Cinnamon Toast

I ate this so much as a kid that I sort of over-dosed on it and stopped eating it for a while, but I have recently rediscovered the cinnamon goodness of this treat!

This one involves toast again. Toast as many pieces as you want. In my case as a kid, I would fill up our toaster, which had four slots. Then butter it and sprinkle sugar and then a little cinnamon on top.

My family loved this treat so much that we filled a sugar bowl with cinnamon and sugar already combined to reduce preparation time from one minute to 30 seconds. Hey, some-times you need cinnamon toast RIGHT NOW! Try it and I'll be willing to bet that you too will have a cinnamon and sugar shaker in your cupboard.

Basic
Boiled Squash

Sound simple enough? Well, it is. Slice your favorite squash and boil, then smother in butter and enjoy. This is much better if you grow your own squash. It's a farm favorite!

Garden
Radishes & Salt

This dish is not for the faint hearted! Pick a few radishes out of the old garden, slice them, and sprinkle with salt. These are a real kick in the pants.

Campfire
Caramel Popcorn

4 cup miniature marshmallows

1 cup brown sugar

1/2 cup butter or margarine

Bring to a boil. After mixture boils for one minute, remove from heat and pour over popped popcorn.

All I can say is, I'm sure that whoever thought to put caramel on popcorn has a guaranteed place in heaven!

Yummy
Fruit Dip

Mix two tablespoons of brown sugar into 1 cup sour cream.

Cut up your favorite fruits and dip!

Perfect for family reunions, at least that's where I always have it.

Green Onion & Cheese
Appetizers

This is one of my grandparent's favorites. I must admit that I haven't been able to get that excited about it yet, but it's an onion lovers dream.

Simply dip the bulb end of a green onion into Cream Cheese, and then roll in grated cheese.

Put a couple on a plate and you have instant appetizers.

TCT's

TCT stands for "Tortilla, Cheese, Tortilla". The rest of the planet probably knows them as quesadillas.

This was a favorite of my family's growing up, and it's really easy. All you do is heat up a frying pan and spray some non-stick cooking spray on it. Lay one flour tortilla down on the pan, and grate cheese on top of it. You can put as much cheese on as you want, but be warned. If you get too much, the cheese starts oozing out the sides and it makes the TCT harder to flip later (believe me, I should know!). After your cheese is grated on top of the first tortilla, you place a second on top of the cheese. Let it sit like that until the cheese starts to melt so that the second tortilla shell sticks to the first. Then flip it over. As soon as the cheese is melted, put your TCT on a plate, cut it pizza style, and enjoy. You can even dip the slices in sour cream and/or salsa.

Frontier Style
Boiled Wheat

This is a hearty snack that had its beginnings in undoubtedly harder times when frontiersmen and pioneers ate whatever they had on hand. The challenge often was cooking it in a way that made it appealing. This way is certainly appealing!

You simply add two parts water to one part wheat and boil until soft. If you add milk and sugar to it, it's a pretty sweet hot cereal.

This snack will keep you going all day whether trying to swim the Great Salt Lake, or pushing a handcart across the prairie.

Here's a pinch more knowledge to add to your Mormon soup...

Roughly 20,000 Mormons made their historic pioneer trek to the West after being driven out of Illinois by violent mobs during the winter of 1845-46.

In February of 1846, with little food, clothing and only provisions they could carry, they were driven from their homes, crossed the Mississippi River into Iowa and camped at a place they called "Winter Quarters," modern-day Florence, Nebraska to try to prepare to come farther west.

They knew that to get relief from their enemies, they would need to go far away from population centers in the Eastern U.S. and that they could expect no help or protection from the government.

Trail-side
Granola Mix

3 cups rolled oats (oatmeal)

1 cup wheat germ

1 or 2 cups raisins, dried currants, or other assorted dried fruits

1/2 cup unsweetened coconut

2 oz. whole sesame seeds

1/2 cup nuts (almonds or cashews are best)

1/2 cup hulled sunflower seeds

1/2 cup olive oil or vegetable oil

1/2 cup honey or molasses

1 tablespoon vanilla

Thoroughly mix all ingredients except fruit and nuts. Spread evenly on cookie sheet and toast for 1 hour, stirring every 15 minutes. Remove from heat and add fruit and nuts. As mixture cools, stir periodically. Serve with milk or yogurt, eat plain as a snack, or store in airtight container.

Pioneer
Baked Beans

3 lbs. pork & beans

1 medium onion, diced

1/2 lb. baked cubed steak

1/2 cup brown sugar

1 cup chili sauce

1 teaspoon dry mustard

Combine all ingredients in cooking pot. Bake at 325° for 3 hours.

Mormon Handcart Pioneers

Thousands of people joined the Mormon Church in Europe in the mid 1800's. Most of these wanted to migrate to the United States to be with the other members.

Because of their poverty, many members booked passage to the U.S. by ship and then made the pioneer journey to the Salt Lake Valley walking over 1000 miles pulling all their belongings in a handcart.

One of the most famous stories in Mormon pioneer history, is that of two heroic young men. A hand cart company left St. Louis late in the season and got caught in early Wyoming snow storms.

They came to a river, which, in the snow, and in their weakened condition made crossing seem overwhelming. They knew they had to hurry because they were getting snowed in and probably would all die from exposure. To their relief, a rescue team, sent by Brigham Young, arrived. Seeing no alternative, two young men from the rescue team began to carry those who were too weak, along with their provisions, across the river on their backs. The two young men carried almost the entire company across the icy cold river – including some of the men.

The two young men suffered health problems for the rest of their lives from the events of that day.

——— \ \ X / / ———

Oatmeal Muffins

1 cup flour

1 cup oatmeal

1 egg

1 cup sour milk

1/2 cup brown sugar

1/2 cup melted shortening

1/2 teaspoon salt

1 teaspoon baking powder

1/2 teaspoon soda

Soak oatmeal in sour milk for one hour. Add egg and beat well. Stir in sugar and shortening.

Add flour which has been sifted with baking powder, salt, and soda. Grease muffin tin and equally divide mix into muffin tin cups. Bake in oven at 400° for 15-20 minutes or until toothpick can be inserted and withdrawn dry. Makes one dozen muffins.

When I think of the Mormon pioneer's, especially the handcart pioneers, struggling across the plains, I remember my own pioneer experience. I myself have experienced a small glimpse into what the pioneers had to endure when I was 18 and went on a small three day pioneer handcart trek.

Now, I considered myself to be in pretty good shape. I work out and play sports, but when I had to pull that handcart over even the smallest of rocks I wondered how the pioneers did it. Amazingly enough, I made it through the three days alive, but about ten pounds lighter because the food was awful and the work was hard. I also ended up with about half as much stuff as I had started out with, because those extra clothes in the hand cart just weren't worth the extra weight and were soon left on the side of the trail.

Oh, by the way, we did have baked beans, but ours were cold out of a can. We were too tired to make food from scratch like the pioneers did.

Original Mormon Pioneer
Soda Biscuits

2 cups flour

1 cup sour cream

1 teaspoon baking powder

1/2 teaspoon salt

Mix all dry ingredients together; add cream, making a soft dough. Knead on floured board. Roll out into 1/2 inch thick. Cut into 2 inch circles. Bake on greased cookie tin at 375 degrees for 15 minutes.

Stick to your ribs all day

Working Pancakes

3/4 cup flour

1/2 cup rolled oats

1 tablespoon sugar

1 teaspoon baking
powder

1/2 teaspoon soda

1/2 teaspoon salt

2 tablespoons oil

1 cup buttermilk

1 egg

As an additional option, add a cup of blue-
berries, apple chunks, or other fruit.

Beat egg. Add the rest of the ingredients and
beat until smooth.

Cook on medium hot griddle being sure the
middle of each pancake is cooked thoroughly.

Grandma Fawn's
Dumplings

Pinch of salt

1 teaspoon baking powder

1 cup flour

1 tablespoon butter

1/2 cup milk

1 egg (optional)

Mix like pie crust

Drop by spoonfuls into boiling chicken soup or broth. Cover, cook until done, about 10 minutes.

V\\//V

It's a joke in our family that we could out-eat any other family in the country. When we all get together there are gargantuan amounts of food, and when we have guests over they are constantly amazed that we can finish it all and still be looking around for something else to eat.

One day we were all sitting around trying to figure out who to blame for our huge appetites and we decided it was all my great grandma, Ora Bundersen Allred's fault. She was just a tiny Danish lady, but she always had tons of good food and she would never believe you were full. My Dad said that when he would go to her house she would heap his plate so full of food that he could barely finish it. Once he had finally got the last bite down and was sitting there trying to keep it down, Grandma would come by and say, "Oh, a growing boy like you can't be full; here, have some more. You look too skinny."

This is one of the recipes from my other grandma, Fawn Duncan, who lived nearby, which my Dad never got to fully enjoy because his stomach was already bulging from being over at Grandma Allred's.

The Relief Society's
5 Cup Salad

1 cup mini marsh-
mallows

1 cup mandarin
oranges, drained

1 cup pineapple
tidbits, drained

1 cup sour cream

1 cup coconut

Mix all together and refrigerate for several hours before serving.

In 1842, Joseph Smith founded the Relief Society. It has become one of the largest women's' organizations in the world.

The Relief Society is famous for having great food at everything they do. Every time they get together or do anything for that matter, it seems that food is involved. One of their favorite activities is the pot luck dinner. At a pot luck dinner, everyone brings a food item of their choice and everyone gets to sample each item.

At some pot luck dinners, sisters (women in the Relief Society are often referred to in Sunday settings as 'Sister' Adams or 'Sister' Thompson, for example) also provide the recipes to their dishes so that those who like them can make them later. Strangely enough, it seems that at least one person always seems to bring this delicious recipe. If by chance you lose it, just head on over to a Relief Society pot luck event near you.

Hotel Utah

Rolls

1 tablespoon yeast or 1 yeast cake

1-1/2 cup boiling water

1-1/2 cubes butter

1/2 cup sugar

1-1/2 teaspoon salt

2 eggs

5 cups flour

Dissolve yeast in 1/4 cup warm water with 1 tsp. sugar. In a pan, bring 1 1/2 cups water to boiling and add butter, 1/2 cup sugar, and salt. Cool. Add beaten eggs and yeast. Add flour and mix well. Let set for 2 hours and rise, then stir it down. Place in refrigerator overnight. It should be sticky; don't knead it.

The next day, roll it out on a lightly floured board into a circle about 1/8" thick and cut into triangles 3 1/2 to 4 inches wide. Spread them with butter, roll them up, and place them on a greased cookie sheet. Let them rise 2 hours. Bake at 400 degrees until golden brown for 15 minutes.

-Thanks to Emily Clark

As you probably know, the largest concentration of Mormons is centered in the state of Utah. (Although this will probably change soon because of the rapid growth of the church in many other countries) Have you ever wondered "why Utah?"

The first group of pioneers were fleeing West, having been driven from New York, Missouri, and Illinois. As the Prophet, Brigham Young came over a ridge into the Salt Lake valley, he knew that this was the place the Lord wanted them to settle because he had seen it in a dream. As the story goes, he stuck his walking stick into the ground and exclaimed, "This is the right place, drive on!"

Today a monument to Brigham Young stands at that spot. Many tourists come every year to visit the monument and also Temple Square, which is one of the top tourists attractions in the world.

In the late 19th century, to accommodate all of these visitors, the Hotel Utah was built. Many changes have filled the years since the hotel was first opened, but Utah still welcomes visitors with warm hospitality just the same.

Polygamist
Potato Pancakes

4 medium potatoes, peeled and grated	1/8 teaspoon nutmeg
Mix together:	1 egg slightly beaten
1 minced onion	1/2 teaspoon salt
2 tablespoons flour	

Add mixture with potatoes and fry in butter. Flatten mounds into 4" circles with pancake turner. Cook approx. 5 minutes. Top with applesauce and sour cream.

Polygamy

I have heard a lot of men jokingly wish out loud that the Mormon church would start practicing polygamy again. Even my fiance has commented on it from time to time. You'd think I would be offended, but I just smile and nod. You see, I know the truth.

I know that most men can only handle one wife and, if it came right down to it, would turn and run (screaming) from the chance to marry a second or third. Think about it, all you men out there, the next time your wife wants you to do the dishes instead of watch TV, or when your six month old baby is up crying all night. Multiply that by 53 and you have an idea of how Brigham Young felt.

The next time you hear some man say how great polygamy would be, just smile and nod like me because you and I know he really couldn't handle it.

The history of Mormon polygamy

As early as 1832, the prophet, Joseph Smith, received the revelation accepting polygamy as a basic doctrine of the church, which was restoring all of the ancient doctrines and practices. This was in perfect harmony with practices of the ancient prophets, such as Abraham, Isaac, Jacob, Moses, and others.

Most Mormons accepted the doctrine reluctantly, since it was so different from their Victorian social principles, but most did as they were asked out of duty and faith.

It is important to know that plural marriage was not open to just anyone who wanted to try it. In Mormon theology, marriage is a sacred institution, which, if performed under priesthood authority can continue through the eternities. Polygamy was only acceptable when it was specifically commanded by the prophet, who held all the keys for sealing on earth and in heaven. Therefore, a man couldn't just arbitrarily decide to take other wives.

This was perfectly okay with most members of the church. Most would much rather have but one wife.

The first wife's consent was usually sought, even if the prophet did extend the call. However, regardless of the couple's personal feelings, their sense of duty and faith usually compelled them to do as asked by the prophet, since they believed he spoke for God.

Once in Utah, the Mormons were isolated from main stream America for a time and allowed to practice with minimal interference; however, as time went on persecution increased.

After decades of persecution and prosecution for the practice, and after appeals to courts failed, President Wilford Woodruff, the prophet at the time, publicly and officially ended the practice in 1898 by issuing "The Manifesto," after seeing in a vision the destruction of his people if the practice continued.

The Allred Family
Broccoli Casserole

2 lbs. broccoli

2 cans cream of chicken soup

2 tablespoons lemon juice

1 cup mayonnaise

3/4 cup bread crumbs

2 teaspoons butter

Cheese

Cook broccoli. Mix soup, lemon juice and mayonnaise into sauce and heat.

Butter pan and place broccoli in it. Pour sauce over broccoli and sprinkle with grated cheese and buttered crumbs. Bake at 350° for 30 minutes.

This is one of our family's favorites, we have it at almost every family gathering, including Thanksgiving. And why not? You have to have at least one casserole at every Mormon gathering.

\\//

Because of the great importance the Mormon Church puts on the family, many families are comparatively large.

My most cherished memories come from times when I was with my family. Every year my family goes on a family reunion. One particular year we decided to go on a trip from Utah to Washington state.

Nine of us, which included my grandparents, my parents, four little kids, and myself piled into a motorhome. I think the trip ended up lasting about two months and consisted mostly of the little kids playing their Game Boys and asking when we were going to be there, about every 2 minutes. While this was going on, my grandmother would occasionally make everyone stop what they were doing and look out the window at the deer.

Now I don't know about you, but to me all deer look pretty much the same. By the end of the trip I was ready to drive the motorhome off a cliff! Strangely, after surviving the ordeal, I now look back on it as one of my fondest memories.

Family Home Evening
Rhubarb Pie

Crust:

2 cups all-purpose flour

1-1/2 Tbs. sugar

1/2 tsp. salt

1/2 cup and 2 Tbs.. butter

1 large egg

2 Tbs. ice water

Mix together the flour, sugar, and salt in a large bowl. Cut the butter in with a pastry cutter. Mix together the egg and water in a small bowl, then add that to the flour/butter mixture. Knead through it with the heal of your hand until it barely holds together. Chill for at least 30 minutes before rolling

Filling:

2 cups rhubarb, diced

3/4 cup sugar

2 tablespoons flour

Nutmeg

Combine above ingredients. Pour into unbaked pie shell. Cover with pie crust.

Bake at 375 degrees for 45 minutes.

Family Home Evening

"Happiness in family life is most likely to be achieved when founded upon the teachings of the Lord Jesus Christ. Successful marriages and families are established and maintained on principles of faith, prayer, repentance, forgiveness, respect, love, compassion, work, and wholesome recreational activities"
("The Family: A Proclamation to the World")

One way that the church helps the family to stay close is by encouraging Mormons to hold "family home evening". It's usually held every Monday night and is a very important part of Mormon culture. At "family home evening" the whole family gets together and has a gospel oriented lesson, does a service project, or just does something fun to strengthen their relationships. In my house we each take turns giving a lesson and then we do some type of activity.

Relief Society
Macaroni Casserole

1 package (8 oz.)
macaroni & cheese
dinner

1 can (6-1/2 oz.)
tuna, drained

1/4 cup chopped
green pepper

1/4 cup sliced pitted
ripe olives

1/4 cup butter or
margarine, melted

1/4 teaspoon garlic
powder

1 cup croutons

Prepare macaroni and cheddar as directed
on package for oven method, except-use 2 1/4
cups water. Stir in tuna, green pepper and
olives. Cover. Bake 20 minutes at 350°.

Blend butter and garlic powder; stir in croutons. Stir casserole and sprinkle croutons over
top. Bake uncovered 5 minutes longer.

Book of Mormon
Meat Pie

Cooked meat (chicken, turkey, hamburger)

1 tablespoon mayonnaise

1-16 oz cottage cheese

Grated mozzarella cheese

Heat all together, then add vegetables. (Frozen peas, carrots, beans, corn, ect. - cooked potatoes)

Pour into uncooked pie crust. Put on top crust. Bake for 30 minutes. at 400-425°.

Grandpa's
Grape Jelly

3-1/2 cups
grape juice

1 pkg. M.C.P. Pectin

4 1/2 cup sugar

1/4 cup lemon juice

Add package of M.C.P. pectin to juice in kettle. Stir well. Place over high heat, bring to a boil, stirring constantly to avoid scorching. Add measured sugar, mix well. Stir constantly and bring to a boil. Boil exactly 2 minutes. Remove from heat. Skim foam off top and pour into bottles.

Now you can try the bread and milk with grape jelly my grandpa loves.

Growing up in a Mormon culture, I often felt I did plenty of service. So, when my parents wanted our family to do more, I wasn't always jumping for joy.

One of the big service projects that my family does each Christmas is making homemade jam and going around to various peoples' houses in our ward and singing Christmas carols and delivering the jam.

Now this was all fine and dandy when I was ten, but I became less and less enthusiastic about the whole idea every year after. One particular year, I was 17 and just assumed that since I was so grown up and independent that my parents wouldn't even consider asking me to participate in such a juvenile ritual as Christmas caroling.

Surprisingly enough, my parents were not all that forward in their thinking and actually told me I had no choice. I begrudgingly handed out jelly and mumbled carols from behind my Dad. At one point while singing "Silent Night" to the family of the captain of the football team, I was ready to make a break for it. Even so, I learned a lot through our service experiences.

Mormon Miracle
Turkey Dressing

1/3 cup margarine

1/4 cup chopped onions

1/3 cup chopped celery

1/2 teaspoon salt

Dash of pepper

3 to 4 cups bread crumbs

Stock from giblets and/or milk to make moist bread

Giblets, cooked

Grind up:

1/4 teaspoon sage

2 apples

Melt butter, add onions and celery to stock, cook until almost done. Add apples, seasonings and giblets. Pour over crumbs. Toss lightly and stuff turkey or steam.

Triple for 12 to 18 pound turkey.

The Seagull Story

Another story that Mormon children grow up hearing is that of the seagulls and the crickets. The pioneers had just settled in the Utah valley and were waiting to harvest their first crop. Then one day a swarm of crickets descended on their crops and began eating them right down to the bare earth. The pioneers tried everything they could, they smashed them, they burned them, they drowned them, but they couldn't get rid of the bugs; there were simply too many.

Finally, to save themselves from ruin, they decided to pray. Soon after their prayers, a huge flock of seagulls appeared and ate all the crickets. The pioneers crops were saved! Because of this great act, the Seagull is Utah's state bird.

--- //\\//\\ ---

Casseroles

As everyone knows, Mormons are famous for their casseroles. We take casseroles to everything, weddings, funerals, birthdays, sporting events, and over to people's houses when they are sick. Because of the extremely high volume of casserole use, and the ease in preparation (you can throw just about anything you have together and call it a casserole) I have devoted a whole section of this book strictly to casserole dishes. If there is one thing we Mormons know, it's that you can never have too many casseroles.

--- //\\//\\ ---

Aunt Augnus's
Artichoke Casserole

1 14-oz. can
artichoke hearts,
drained

1 6-oz. bag
stuffing mix

1 15-oz. can french
cut green beans,
drained

1 14-oz. can
chicken broth

1 8-oz. can
sliced mushrooms,
drained

1 cup grated
parmesan cheese

2 teaspoon
garlic powder

1/4 cup olive oil

Preheat oven to 350 degrees. Cut artichoke hearts into quarters and place in large bowl. Add remaining ingredients; Mix well. Pour into 2 quart baking dish. Bake, uncovered, 30 minutes or until heated through.

Sunday Stuffing & Summer
Squash Casserole

1 6-oz. bag
seasoned stuffing

5 cups sliced yellow
summer squash or
zucchini

1 10-oz. can cream
of mushroom soup

1/2 cup sour cream

1 tablespoon
minced onions

1/4 teaspoon
black pepper

Preheat oven to 350 degrees. Prepare stuffing mix according to package directions, except reduce water to 3/4 cup. Spread half of the prepared stuffing in 2 quart baking dish. In large saucepan cook squash and carrot, covered, in small amount of boiling water 8 to 10 minutes or until tender. Drain well. Stir in soup, sour cream, minced onions, and pepper. Spoon vegetable mixture over stuffing. Top with remaining stuffing. Bake 35 to 40 minutes or until heated through.

"Oh my Gosh!"

Green Bean Casserole

1 10-oz. can cream of mushroom soup

1/2 cup milk

1 teaspoon soy sauce

dash pepper

4 cups cooked cut green beans

1-1/3 cups french fried onions

Mix soup, milk, soy sauce, pepper, beans and 2/3 cup onions in 1-1/2 qt. casserole dish. Bake at 350 degrees for 25 minutes or until hot.

Stir, then sprinkle with remaining onions. Bake another 5 minutes.

Girl's Camp Crab &
Shrimp Casserole

1 cup wild rice, cooked

1 pound shrimp

1/2 pound fresh mushrooms, sliced

3 tablespoons butter

2 13-oz. cans artichoke hearts, drained & chopped

1 pound fresh crab meat, cleaned

1/2 red bell pepper, chopped

1/2 cup chopped onion

1 cup chopped celery

1 cup mayonnaise

3/4 cup light cream

1 tablespoon Worcestershire sauce

salt and ground pepper to taste

Cook shrimp in boiling salted water until barely pink. Drain. Remove shells. Sauté mushrooms in butter until tender, about 5 minutes. Combine shrimp, mushrooms and all remaining ingredients. Pour into large ungreased casserole dish. Bake uncovered at 375 degrees for 30 minutes, or until hot and bubbly.

Big
Black Bean Casserole

1 tablespoon oil

1 medium onion, chopped

1 clove garlic, minced

2 15-oz. cans black beans, drained

1 10-oz. can tomatoes with green chilies

1 4-oz. can diced mild chilies

2 tablespoons fresh cilantro chopped

salt and freshly ground pepper to taste

9 corn tortillas, each cut into 6 sections

1-1/2 cups Mozzarella cheese, shredded

1/2 cup cheddar cheese, shredded

In a saucepan, sauté onion and garlic in oil. Add beans, tomatoes, chilies, cilantro, and salt and pepper. Simmer 10 minutes. In a 2 quart buttered casserole dish layer 1/3 tortillas, 1/3 beans, and 1/3 cheese., Continue layering, and end with cheeses. Cover and bake at 375 degrees for 20 minutes. Uncover and bake 15 minutes longer until cheese is browned.

Vidalia
Onion Casserole

8 medium vidalia
onions, chopped

4 ounces butter,
melted

2 eggs

1 12-oz. can
evaporated milk

1 cup grated
Parmesan cheese

salt and pepper to
taste

8 oz. Monterey Jack
cheese, shredded

In a non-stick saucepan, cook onions with
1/2 cup water until tender. Pour hot onions
over butter in shallow casserole dish. Mix
together eggs, milk, Parmesan cheese, salt,
pepper and half the Monterey Jack cheese.
Pour sauce over onions, and sprinkle with
remaining Monterey Jack cheese on top. Bake
at 350 degrees for 30 minutes.

Hashbrown Casserole

1 10-oz. can cream
of celery soup

1-3/4 cups milk

1/2 cup sour cream
with chives

3 tablespoons
chopped onion

1 package hash-
browns with onions

2 tablespoons
chopped green
pepper

1/2 teaspoon salt

1/8 teaspoon pepper

Heat oven to 350 degrees. Mix soup, milk,
sour cream, onion, green pepper, salt and pepper. Stir in potatoes. Pour into ungreased baking dish, 8x8x2 inches. Bake uncovered 50 to
60 minutes or until tender.

Summary

One of the fundamental beliefs that set Mormons apart from the rest of the world, and make them so healthy, is a passage of scripture known as the Word of Wisdom. Mormon cooking is unique because of it. The Word of Wisdom is a revelation received by Joseph Smith, the first latter-day prophet of the church, in 1836, which advises against consumption of tobacco, alcohol, and hot drinks, (since defined as coffee and tea). The Word of Wisdom also recommends limiting the consumption of meat, and encourages the use of whole grains, fresh fruits and vegetables. Thanks to adherence to this law, recent findings show that Utah enjoys the lowest rates of death due to cancer and heart disease in the United States.

Mormons also believe that all people are literal sons and daughters of God. As such, we must honor our heavenly parents. One of the ways we do this is by taking care of our bodies. Following the Word of Wisdom is an important part of this.

Hopefully, this book has answered some of your questions about Mormons, and corrected some of the misconceptions that are out there. If not, at least you have some great new recipes to try, and who knows, maybe you really will like that green Jell-O with grated cheese recipe – if you are brave enough to try it!

Order these additional Cookbooks from The American Pantry Collection

Order Online! www.apricotpress.com

Apricot Press Order Form

Book Title	Quantity	x	Cost / Book	=	Total

All Cook Books are $9.95 US.

Do not send Cash. Mail check or
money order to:
**Apricot Press   P.O. Box 1611
American Fork, Utah   84003**
Telephone 801-756-0456
Allow 3 weeks for delivery.

**Quantity discounts available.
Call us for more information.**
9 a.m. - 5 p.m. MST

Sub Total =

Shipping = $2.00

Tax 8.5% =

Total Amount
Enclosed =

Shipping Address

Name:

Street:

City: State:

Zip Code:

Telephone:

Email: